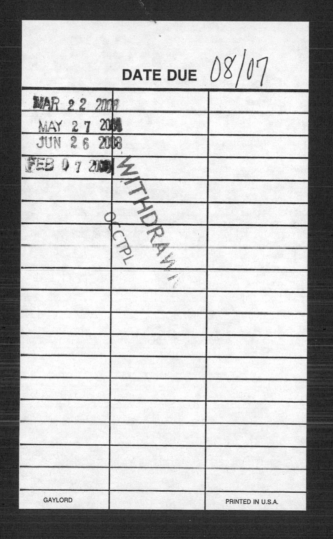

GETTING TO KNOW
THE U.S. PRESIDENTS

GEORGE W.
BUSH

FORTY-THIRD PRESIDENT
2001 – PRESENT

WRITTEN AND ILLUSTRATED BY MIKE VENEZIA

CHILDREN'S PRESS
AN IMPRINT OF SCHOLASTIC INC.
NEW YORK   TORONTO   LONDON   AUCKLAND   SYDNEY
MEXICO CITY   NEW DELHI   HONG KONG
DANBURY, CONNECTICUT

Reading Consultant: Nanci R. Vargus, Ed.D., Assistant Professor, School of Education, University of Indianapolis

Historical Consultant: Marc J. Selverstone, Ph.D., Assistant Professor, Miller Center of Public Affairs, University of Virginia

Photographs © 2008: AP/Wide World Photos: 27 (Tech Sgt. Cedric H. Rudisill/Department of Defense), 17 (The White House); Aurora Photos/Robb Kendrick: 21; Corbis Images: 31 (Peter Andrews/Reuters), 7 (Yoni Brook), 26 (U.S. Fish and Wildlife Service/Reuters), 32 (Rick Wilking/Reuters), 22 (David Woo/Dallas Morning News); Department of Defense/Eric Draper/White House: 3; George Bush Presidential Library: 8, 10, 12, 14, 18, 19; Getty Images: 20 (Cynthia Johnson), 28 (Paul J. Richards/AFP), 4 (Stock Montage); Index Stock Imagery/Maps.com: 29; Landov, LLC: 5 (Normand Blouin/UPI), 30 (Desmond Boylan/Reuters).

Colorist for illustrations: Andrew Day

Library of Congress Cataloging-in-Publication Data

Venezia, Mike.
  George W. Bush / written and illustrated by Mike Venezia.
      p. cm. — (Getting to know the U.S. presidents)
  ISBN-13: 978-0-516-22649-1 (lib. bdg.)   978-0-516-25595-8 (pbk.)
  ISBN-10: 0-516-22649-5 (lib. bdg.)   0-516-25595-9 (pbk.)
  1. Bush, George W. (George Walker), 1946—Juvenile literature. 2.
Presidents—United States—Biography—Juvenile literature. I. Title.
  E903.V46 2008
  973.931092—dc22
  [B]
                                        2006102975

President
George W. Bush

George W. Bush, the forty-third president of the United States, was born in New Haven, Connecticut, on July 6, 1946. George W. Bush was only the second person in history whose father had also been a U.S. president. The first George Bush served as president twelve years before his son.

Because the first President Bush and second President Bush have the same name, it's easy to get them confused.

John Quincy Adams (left) was the sixth U.S. president. His father, John Adams (right), was the second U.S. president.

Over the years, news writers and Bush family members have come up with ways to keep people from getting the two presidents mixed up.

Former President George Bush waves with his son, President George W. Bush

When George W. Bush started out as president in January of 2001, things were going along pretty well in the nation. President Bush had plans to take care of things at home in the United States. These plans included cutting taxes, exploring for new energy sources, improving public school systems, and getting members of the government to cooperate more with each other.

Then, on September 11, 2001, something happened that changed President Bush's life and the lives of all Americans forever. On that day, terrorists from the Middle East took over four U.S. passenger planes. They crashed two of the planes into the World Trade Center towers in New York City.

A firefighter searches for survivors at the site of the World Trade Center on September 12, 2001.

Another plane was flown into the Pentagon, the nation's defense headquarters in Washington, D.C. The fourth passenger jet crashed in a wooded field in Pennsylvania. More than 3,000 lives were lost that day. Now President Bush would spend most of his time working to protect the United States and fighting terrorism.

George W. Bush, at about the age of nine, while on a trip with his dad to the oil fields in Midland, Texas

George W. Bush came from a pretty wealthy family. His father was part owner of a successful oil company. Even so, the younger George grew up mainly in Midland, Texas. Midland was an everyday, working-class town, next to hot, dusty Texas oil fields.

George loved playing baseball more than anything. He had one of the best baseball card collections around. George W.'s idol was Willie Mays, a New York Giants superstar. George probably could have gotten better grades. Instead of doing his homework, he spent too much time memorizing the names and positions of major-league ball players.

George W. Bush (center) with his grandmother Dorothy Walker Bush (left), his younger sister Robin, and his father, George H. W. Bush, in 1953

George W. Bush had a happy childhood growing up in Midland. There was one event, though, that caused George and his parents the greatest sadness of all. When George was only seven, his four-year-old sister, Robin, died of a blood disease called leukemia. George was devastated.

When George saw how sad his parents were, though, he started to do whatever he could to cheer them up. George W. became kind of a clown at home. He also became a jokester at school, even if it meant getting in trouble. George once painted Elvis Presley-type sideburns on his face to get a laugh. His teacher then marched him down to the principal's office, where he got a whacking!

George W. Bush used his excellent sense of humor to attract friends all through school. When George was in eighth grade, his family moved to Houston, Texas. George entered a fancy private school there. Then he went to a private high school in Massachusetts. For college, George attended Yale University in Connecticut. Yale was the same college George's father and grandfather had attended.

George W. Bush at Yale University

Both of the senior Bushes were still remembered at Yale for their excellent grades and athletic achievements. The young George W. Bush did OK in school and in sports, but he was remembered more for the great parties he threw. George W. was a genius at making friends and having fun. This talent would help him a lot later, when he got into politics.

George W. Bush in front of his Texas National Guard fighter plane

After graduating from Yale in 1968, George joined the Texas National Guard. At this time, the United States was involved in a war in Vietnam. Because George enlisted in the National Guard and not the U.S. Army, there was very little chance he would be sent to fight in Vietnam. Later, when he was running for president, critics would say George joined the Guard to avoid going to Vietnam.

George W. Bush said he just wanted to learn to be a fighter pilot like his father had been during World War II. George learned to fly an F-102 fighter jet. During his time off, he continued to party and have as much fun as possible. After a while, though, George realized he would have to get serious about what to do with the rest of his life.

George decided to go to Harvard Business School. After Harvard, he returned to Midland and started up an oil company. He called it Arbusto, which is Spanish for "Bush." George wasn't as lucky finding oil as his father had been, and Arbusto Oil Company didn't do very well.

George thought he might do better in politics. He decided to run for Congress. During this time, George W. Bush met the love of his life. At a backyard barbeque party, George was introduced to Laura Welch, a school librarian. It was love at first sight! After dating for just three months, George and Laura got married.

On their wedding day, George W. and Laura Bush pose with George's parents.

Marrying Laura was the best thing to happen to George. Laura helped him campaign when he ran for Congress. Because George really wasn't that well known to voters, he lost his first election. He did learn a lot about campaigning and politics, though. Laura's love and support made the loss much easier to take.

George and Laura Bush campaign for Congress from the back of a pickup truck in 1978.

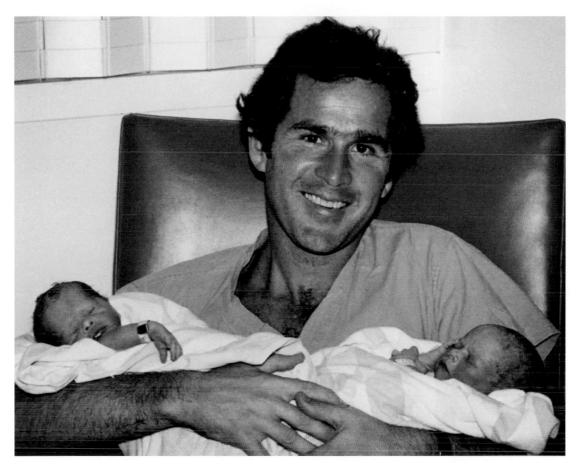
George W. Bush holds his newborn twin daughters, Barbara and Jenna, in 1981.

In 1981, Laura gave birth to twin girls.
George was a family man now, but he still
spent a lot of time partying. Finally, Laura
convinced him life was too important to waste.
George agreed. He stopped drinking alcohol
and became more closely connected to his
Christian faith. Soon, George W. Bush's life
began to change for the better.

When George H. W. Bush ran for president in 1988, George W. (above) helped campaign for him.

George was able to concentrate on more important things now. When George's father ran for president, George and Laura moved to Washington, D.C. George became an important campaign advisor. He used his humor and talent for making friends to help his father win the election.

After the election, George moved back to Texas. He decided to sell his oil company and use the money to become part owner of the Texas Rangers baseball team. George helped the Rangers become a successful team. He even put his own picture on a baseball card!

Texas Rangers part-owner George W. Bush at Texas Stadium in Arlington, Texas

Texans got a chance to get to know George better when he helped run the Rangers. George was always making public appearances and being interviewed on news programs. When it came time to elect the governor of Texas, George decided to run for the job.

Governor George W. Bush autographs a baseball for a Texas Rangers fan at Texas Stadium in 1998.

George Bush belonged to the Republican political party. He ran against Democratic governor Ann Richards. Being a popular baseball club owner really helped George. His campaign promises pleased voters, and he won the election in 1994.

As governor, George Bush was able to get political opponents to work together. He signed laws to make neighborhoods safer, improve schools, and help poor people in his state.

George Bush was such a successful governor that Republican Party members asked him to run for president. George accepted the offer. In 2000, he ran against the Democratic candidate, Al Gore. The election of 2000 was one of the closest, most complicated elections in American history. At the end of Election Day, only a few hundred votes in Florida separated the two candidates.

At first, George Bush had the lead. But
Democrats believed there were votes in Florida
that hadn't been counted, or were counted
incorrectly. They demanded that thousands of
votes be recounted. Over the next few weeks,
Bush and Gore supporters bickered back and
forth. Finally, the U.S. Supreme Court stopped
the recount, and George W. Bush became the
next president of the United States.

The Senate blocked President Bush's plan to drill for oil in the Arctic National Wildlife Refuge.

Soon after his inauguration, President Bush recommended cutting federal income taxes. At this time, the U.S. government had a lot of money for the first time in years. The president thought some of that money should be returned to taxpayers. President Bush and his advisors also recommended drilling for oil in Alaskan wildlife areas.

With the support of many Democrats, the president signed a law to help improve the nation's educational system. While some of President Bush's ideas seemed good for the nation, others didn't. This caused a lot of arguments and disagreements in Congress. Then, on September 11, 2001, terrorists attacked the United States, and everything changed.

The Pentagon in Washington, D.C., after the 9/11 attack

President Bush speaks to firefighters and other workers at the site of the destroyed World Trade Center on September 14, 2001.

For a short time, people in the United States and members of the government put their differences aside. When it was discovered that a terrorist organization, called al-Qaeda, was responsible for the attack, President Bush acted with great force. He gathered support and worked with other countries to send troops to Afghanistan, where al-Qaeda members were

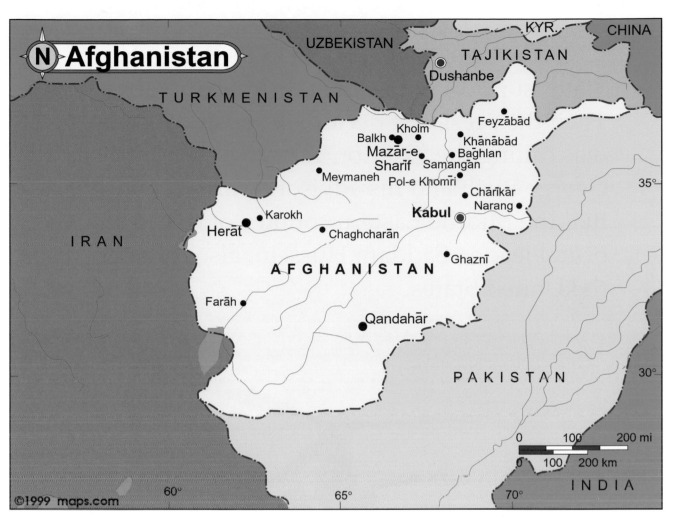

A map of Afghanistan and the surrounding region

hiding. In Afghanistan, the United States and its allies attacked al-Qaeda and the Taliban government that protected them. President Bush said that from then on the United States would not only fight terror groups wanting to harm America, but also any country that was willing to help them.

At the time, most people in the United States supported President Bush's decisions. Then the president decided to push what he was calling the "War on Terror" a step further. George Bush and his advisors were convinced that the Middle Eastern country of Iraq, and its brutal leader, Saddam Hussein, also threatened the United States.

A helicopter drops U.S. Marines into the Iraqi desert during the Iraq War in March 2003.

Iraqi citizens stand happily on top of a statue of Saddam Hussein that had been toppled by U.S. led forces in the town of Kerbala, Iraq, in April 2003.

Over the objections of many world leaders, President Bush ordered the invasion of Iraq. American troops easily defeated the Iraqi army and drove Saddam from power. The Iraqis were able to write a constitution and form a new democratic government. Yet many American troops are still risking their lives in Iraq fighting Iraqi and foreign insurgents.

Laura and George W. Bush relaxing on their ranch in Crawford, Texas

Even though many people disagreed with the war in Iraq, George Bush won a second term as president in 2004. But as the war dragged on, President Bush's policies became more and more unpopular. Still, George W. Bush believes that if Iraq's new government is successful, peace can spread throughout the Middle East.